There Is Greatness Within You, My Son

There Is Greatness Within You, My Son

A collection of poems

Blue Mountain Press ®

SPS Studios ™
Boulder, Colorado

Library of Congress Catalog Card Number:
ISBN: 0-88396-396-5

ACKNOWLEDGMENTS appear on page 64.

 design on book cover is registered in
U.S. Patent and Trademark Office.

Manufactured in the United States of America
Sixth Printing: January 2000

This book is printed on recycled paper.

Library of Congress Cataloging-in-Publication Data

There is greatness within you, my son : a collection of poems from
    Blue Mountain Arts.
        p.   cm.
      ISBN 0-88396-396-5
      1. Mothers and sons—Poetry. 2. Fathers and sons—Poetry.
    3. American poetry—20th century. I. Blue Mountain Arts (Firm)
    PS595.M66T48   1994
    811'.54080920441—dc20   94-31218
                                                        CIP

This book is printed on fine quality, laid embossed, 80 lb. paper. This paper
has been specially produced to be acid free (neutral pH) and contains no
groundwood or unbleached pulp. It conforms with all of the requirements of
the American National Standards Institute, Inc., so as to ensure that this book
will last and be enjoyed by future generations.

SPS Studios, Inc.
P.O. Box 4549, Boulder, Colorado 80306

CONTENTS

I'm So Proud
of You, My Son

When I held you as a child,
it was like taking up in my arms
all of my hopes for the future.
I loved you so much then
that I felt my heart would break
with the pride and joy I felt.
I wondered then who you would become,
and you haven't let me down.

You are a person to be proud of.
You are sensitive, but strong,
with the courage to follow your own path,
to know and do what is right for you.
The love between us needs few words,
but is the foundation for all we give
by being there, by sharing time and effort,
by our talks, and by our caring.
I'm proud when you accomplish things,
but even prouder of the way you live.
Whether you win or lose,
you do it with integrity and humanity,
and I respect that.
From your own efforts, there has grown
a deep goodness in you.
I can wish nothing more
than that your life will hold a future
of happiness.

— Ruthann Tholen

Remember These Things, Son...

Always keep your many interests —
they will keep you
constantly occupied
Always keep your positive outlook —
it will give you the energy to
accomplish great things
Always keep your determination —
it will give you the ability
to succeed in meeting your goals
Always keep your excitement
about whatever you do —
it will help you to have fun
Always keep your sense of humor —
it will allow you to
make mistakes and learn from them

Always keep your confidence —
it will allow you to take risks
and not be afraid of failure
Always keep your sensitivity —
it will help you to understand
and do something about
injustices in the world
As you continue to grow
in your own unique, wonderful way
always remember that
I am more proud of you
than ever before and
I love you

— Susan Polis Schutz

A son is a first smile that you
never forget.
He's tiny footsteps that fill your heart
with pride.
He's skinned knees and messy hair,
as well as pride and frustration.
A son can be grown-up and mature,
yet still be your little boy:
a child and an adult rolled into one.
As he becomes an adult, you see
the love you have given him
passed on and shared.
And he blesses your life by proving
to be the type of man
you always hoped and prayed
he'd grow up to be.

— Barbara Cage

Son, I Want to Give You the Gifts That Last Forever

I want to give you
the kinds of gifts that will last
your whole life through,
things that you just
can't put a price tag on.
I want to give you
the courage to
stand up for what you believe in;
a level head;
   a warm heart;
a sense of humor
to get you through any situation;
the ability to keep
growing and learning
as life brings changes;
a positive outlook for the future;
the love and support
of friends and family;
and the confidence
   and inspiration
to follow your dreams
wherever they may
   take you.

— Morgan R. Gray

I Want to Thank You
for the Gifts You Have
Given Me

In your lifetime, you have given me
far more gifts than I can count;
yet the ones I remember most are
the ones you gave from within,
often without even realizing it.
As a child, you gave me the gift
of allowing me to see the world
through your eyes, and finding beauty
I had overlooked before.
The many memories we've made,
the love you have given,
    and the love I have for you
are lifetime gifts.
I want to thank you for all
    you've given me,
and let you know that
    one of the greatest gifts of all
is the joy that has been mine
    ever since the moment
        I first held you in my arms.

— Deanne Laura Gilbert

To You, Son,
with a Lot of Love

Sometimes we need
reminders in our lives
of how much
    people care.

If you ever get that feeling,
    I want you to remember this...

I love you, Son.

Beyond words that can even begin
to tell you how much,
    I hold you and your happiness
        within my heart each and
            every day.

I am so proud of you, and so thankful
to the years that have given me
so much to be thankful for.

    If I were given a chance to be
    anything I wanted to become,
    there's nothing I would rather be
        ...than your parent.

            And there is no one
            I would rather have
            ...as my son.

— Laurel Atherton

Always Believe in Yourself, Son, and Remember That Anything Is Possible

Believe in what makes you feel good.
Believe in what makes you happy.
Believe in the dreams
  you've always wanted to come true,
    and give them every chance to.

Life holds no promises
  as to what will come your way.
You must search for your own ideals
  and work towards reaching them.
Life makes no guarantees
  as to what you'll have.
It just gives you time to make choices
  and to take chances
and to discover whatever secrets
  might come your way.

If you are willing to take
   the opportunities you are given
     and utilize the abilities you have,
you will constantly fill your life
   with special moments
     and unforgettable times.

No one knows the mysteries of life
   or its ultimate meaning,
but for those who are willing
   to believe in their dreams
     and in themselves,
life is a precious gift
   in which anything is possible.

                — Dena Dilaconi

Whatever You Choose
to Do with Your Life,
I Will Be Proud of You

It is so important
to choose your own
lifestyle
and not let others
choose it for you
Do what you want to do
Be what you want to be
Look the way you want to look
Act the way you want to act
Think the way you want to think
Speak the way you want to speak
Follow the goals you want to follow

Live according to the truths
   within yourself
and know that whatever you do
I am here to support you
and always feel very proud of you

— Susan Polis Schutz

I'll Always Care
About Your Happiness

I realize that it isn't always easy for you
to open up to me about your life
and matters you may consider
too personal to share.
Perhaps because we are parent and child,
there are natural barriers
that stand between us
and make it difficult for us to communicate.
I can understand how you may believe
that we are too different,
and our places in life
too far removed from each other,
for me to be able to understand you.
Yet it is because I am your parent
that I try so hard to understand.

I can't read your mind or claim to know
all that you feel and experience
at any given time.
Yet I can remember my own trials at your age.
I won't tell you that I have all the answers
or that I always know what is right for you.
But because I love you,
I care about your happiness and well-being.
Because I am your parent,
there is a natural instinct that urges me
to protect you from any harm or pain
and a strong desire to remain
a part of your life.
I would like for you to remember
that I am always here for you.
And during the times when you aren't able
or don't feel comfortable enough
to approach me,
simply remember that I love you.

— Katherine J. Romboldi

You're an original, an
individual, a masterpiece.
Celebrate that; don't let
your uniqueness make you shy.
Don't be someone other than
the wonder you are. Every
star is important to the sky.

— Alin Austin

There was always something special
about you. The average and ordinary
were never enough. You had to climb
a little farther, reach a little higher.
While some dreamed dreams, wishing
they would come true, you worked hard
making your dreams a reality. While
others hoped, you tried, and most often
succeeded. I wanted you to know how
proud I am of all you have accomplished,
of all you have become.

— M. Joye

BE YOURSELF!

This is the best and only
person you can be.
Don't take away from your uniqueness
by trying to change it.
Being yourself leads to success.
Being someone you are not, to failure.
Use your time and energy
to make the most of who you are —
to build yourself up,
not tear yourself down.

BE YOURSELF!
Care about and consider the feelings
of those closest to you,
but don't allow others to tell you
how to think, feel, be, or live.
Only you have the right
to make these important decisions.

BE YOURSELF!
If others reject you,
don't be hard on yourself.
Their rejection has nothing to do
with who you are;
it has to do with who they are.

BE YOURSELF!

Be honest, because if you aren't,
it will be impossible for you
to feel good about yourself, and
for others to feel good about you.
Self-respect begins with honesty;
the respect of others comes
as a result of your own respect for yourself.

BE YOURSELF!

Accept yourself as being imperfect,
but not unlovable,
for your strengths
far exceed any weaknesses.
Embrace the goodness in you;
there is more there than you acknowledge.

BE YOURSELF!

You are a part of the universe,
not by accident, but by design.
You have a special place and purpose.
Trust your creator.
There's a star in the sky
with your name on it.
Claim that star and let it shine.
For you...
for others...
for a world whose survival depends on light...
let it shine.

— Nancye Sims

Don't Ever Give Up
on Your Dreams

There may be times when you feel as if you have taken a million steps towards your dreams, and acted on your plans, only to find yourself in the same place that you began from. At times like this, you must not give up.

When you feel as if all that you have strived after and worked for has failed, you must continue on. Though you feel lost, bewildered, and alone, continue to believe in yourself. If you allow discouragement and doubt to blur your vision and wash away your dreams, then you will be left with nothing. Visualize your way beyond the detours, standstills, and obstacles.

You will realize your dreams. When someone has worked as hard as you have and taken so many productive steps in a positive direction, they will succeed. Whatever the hurt of the moment may be, it will pass. Tomorrow is always a new dawn. Today, you must pause, rest, catch your breath, and then look ahead. Each step will bring you closer to your dreams.

— Vicki Silvers

Work Hard, Son...
but Have Fun, Too

It's important to be serious
about your goals,
but I'm hoping you'll also remember
the enjoyable side of life.
Include some time-outs in your busy schedule;
don't let life rush by.
I'm hoping your quests will be successful,
but I'd also like to see you
spending good times with friends,
making special moments,
and doing things you want to do just
for the pleasure it brings to your heart.

Do the things that make you happy
to be you;
You are living in a world filled
with opportunities for good things in life.
Stay as special as you are
and as filled with hopes and dreams
    as you are today,
but please keep that boyish grin in place,
and always remember to make special room
for happiness in your life —
the kind that keeps you in touch
with your friends, your dreams,
and the world around you.
I'm very proud of you,
and I'll always be wishing for
    your greatest happiness.

— Barbara J. Hall

Be the Best You Can Be, and Be Happy!

Think of the future as a wonderful
    door opening into a promising new land.
Learn from the past,
    but do not let it determine your future.
Forget about any past mistakes.
Be glad that you are living in a world
    that is so full of opportunity. Be optimistic.
Appreciate the fact that you have God-given
    talents and abilities that are uniquely yours,
and don't be afraid to use them.
Seek the advice and help of others,
but always remember that
    yours is the final word.
Make your own decisions,
explore your own self,
find your own dreams.
Be persistent; try not to get discouraged
    when things don't go your way.
Do all that you can to make this world
    a better place to live.
Be aware that life isn't always easy,
    but that given time and hard work,
    it can be everything you want it to be.
Most of all, be happy!
The future awaits you,
    and it's a wonderful time to be alive.

— MacKenzie Sinclair

Make Every Day of Your Life
an Adventure

For some, life is an adventure:
an adventure of the spirit
and of the body.

Each new day
begins with wonder and anticipation
for the newness that the day will offer.
It will bring opportunities for
growth,
love,
passion for being, and
the inner search for understanding.

Each day is unique, like a solitary snowflake
searching for itself and its place among the
millions of snowflakes that
have ventured on ahead of it.
Each new day adds color to the tapestry
of a well-lived life
and music to a carefree soul.

Each new experience blends to create a life
of purpose and passion
that shines like a lighthouse, sending its light
miles out to sea to guide weary or lost travelers
home to safety and the meaning
of their lives.

We are all here for a very short time.
The plan of this universe offers its share of
surprises and twists of destiny that curse the timid soul.
But those who live life as an adventure welcome
these turns in the road and quirks of fate.
For them, each day is packed full of as many sights and
sounds and tastes and emotions as they can experience.

For some, life is drudgery. It reeks of sameness
and routine, gray skies, dull sounds, bland people, and
suppressed emotions.

We make our days; they don't make us.
To live a life full of
adventure, learn to laugh more,
feel more,
share more,
learn more, and love more.

— Tim Connor

This I ask of you, my son —
That you strive to be all that you can be,
    yet never become a copy of another
That you realize your own unique qualities,
    and all that makes you special
That you open your eyes to the beauty
    in each day
That you reach out to others less fortunate
    than you
That, by giving, you learn the joy of
    receiving
That you let go of the sadness of the past,
    yet always remember the good moments
That you learn to accept life as it is,
    even with its problems and disappointments
For life is meant to be enjoyed
    and, at times, endured, but never taken
    for granted
Just be aware at all times
    that you are one special person,
    among all special persons
And do the best you can.

— Rhoda-Katie Hannan

When you dream, dream deep.
When you love, make it last.
When you have hopes, hold on
to them with all your heart.
Your possibilities are unsurpassed.

When you share, share completely.
When thoughts wander, let them soar.
When your wishes come up empty,
don't give up on them. Your
opportunities might be just behind
the next door.

When you deal with difficulties, keep
your courage. When you awaken,
remember that each sunrise is brand-new.
When you travel towards tomorrow, choose
your own direction. Your happiness will
always help to guide you.

When special feelings come your way,
let them flow into your heart. When
miracles try to find you, don't hide.
When special people come along, let
them know what a blessing they are.
Smiles begin way down, deep inside.

— Collin McCarty

Never Underestimate
Your Abilities

You can do all you're dreaming of.
Don't let those little doubts appear;
dismiss them from your mind.
You're so strong and capable;
you're brave and willing, too.
You have so many reasons to succeed,
so much in your favor,
and so much going for you.
Don't minimize your keen abilities
or deprive your dreams
of great fulfillment.
Recognize your strengths.
Adopt a positive approach.
Assert your powers of positive thinking.
Stay in control.
Above all, think you can,
believe you can,
and most certainly you will!

— Barbara J. Hall

How Can You Measure the Value of a Man?

The measure of a man is not found in
the things he owns,
or what he's saved for retirement,
or even his accomplishments.

The true measure of a man is found in
his faith and his heart.
It's found in the friends who stand by him,
the strength he displays under pressure,
the sensitivity he unashamedly expresses,
and his willingness to reveal vulnerability,
even at the risk of being hurt.

And it's found in the truth of his words,
the genuineness of his life,
his unselfish actions,
and the values he lives by.

Determine the measure of a man
not by admiring his trophies
or by comparing him to other men
who are either weaker or stronger.

Determine the measure of a man
by how much you trust him
and believe in him,
and by how much his life enhances yours.

— Craig Brannon

As You Go
Through Life, Son...

Don't forget your self-confidence. When
you rise in the morning and prepare for
the day, ready your strength, for you will
always need it. Hang on to your convictions,
for they are what make you different. Give
yourself credit for being intelligent and capable.

Don't forget your compassion. When you
look at yourself in the mirror, study your face
carefully. Look for the courage to believe in
yourself. Find the will to face the day ahead.
Know that you are human and therefore
capable of failing.

Don't forget your hope. When you are certain
there is none left, look deep inside. There you
will find faith in yourself and those you love.
There you will find belief that tomorrow will come.
There you will find comfort in knowing that you
are loved by those closest to you.

Don't forget your charity. When you feel
that there could be no pain greater than yours,
look around you. Recognize that someone
before you has suffered greater. Know that
someone after you will suffer more. Realize
that pain is relative to everyone everywhere.

Don't forget your laughter. When reasoning
fails you and logic drifts far away, look to
your heart. It is there you will find the humor
in life and your ability to laugh out loud at
yourself without fearing criticism. Remember
that there is more medicine in a laugh
than in a tear.

Don't forget who you are.
Don't forget the part that is humane,
the part that is hopeful,
or the part that is charitable.
And never forget the laughter.

— Chris Marie Perrin

If Someone Asked Me
to Define the Perfect Son,
I Would Say...

"Search for a young man whose heart
   is as big as the Grand Canyon;
search for a young man who thinks
   only of others;
search for a young man who does
   a thousand good deeds each day
      while expecting nothing in return;
search for a young man who suffers
   and never complains.
And when your search is over,
   if you have found such a young man,
then rejoice —
   for you have found my son."

— Jeffrey K. Lucas

I Wish for You,
My Son,
the Greatest Things
in Life

I wish you Love: unconditional
and unending.
I wish you Understanding:
an open mind, a caring heart,
and answers to all of your questions.
I wish you Determination:
to go after what you want, make it
work, and do the right thing.
I wish you Faith: to believe
in yourself, to trust your abilities, and
to keep on trying.
I wish you Peace: the ability to
forgive, calmness in stressful
times, and the comfort of love.

I wish you Fulfillment: enough time to
do what you enjoy, someone to share
the good times with, the ability
to recognize when something isn't
working, and the courage to move on.
I wish you Joy: a sense of humor, a
hand to hold, and pride in what
you do.
I wish you Gentleness: in touching,
feeling, and experiencing everything.
I wish you Goodness: honesty, integrity,
and loyalty not only from others,
but from within yourself as well.
I wish you Patience: in your actions,
your words, and your quest to become
all that you can be.

— Barbara Cage

You have so many moments
ahead of you, Son...
days that will bring new people
into your life, and times that will
bring new friends into your world.

Having had the wonderful pleasure
of knowing you (since the minute
you were born!) and appreciating
the million and one things that
are so wonderful about you...

I will always hope that the people
who share your life are
special, insightful people who
realize how lucky they are
to be in the presence
of a present
like you.

— Marta Best

It Is All Up to You, Son, to Make Your Dreams Come True

If you believe in your dreams, and work hard and long towards making them part of your reality, then more than likely you'll achieve whatever dreams you want to come true.

When you believe in something and focus your time and talents towards fulfilling that belief, then as time passes, you will be continually traveling in the right direction. If you have a positive attitude about your life, you have almost everything that you'll ever need. Hope, faith, and believing in good things will lead you on the right path to happiness and success.

Challenges will come into your life, but the way that you perceive them will determine how positive or negative they will be in relationship to your life. If you accept a certain amount of disappointment, and strive to replace it with optimism and hope, then it will be a strengthening element in your life.

The simple keys to life are those that you, yourself, must turn. They are the ones that tell you to expect happiness as well as change, and to make the most out of every day. Be ready to make your dreams come true, because it is all up to you.

— Dena Dilaconi

Son, You Are
the Artist of Your Life

You truly are a blessed individual in life. You are gifted with an endless array of wonderful talents and opportunities, and a strong awareness of the importance of being you.

Take the time to discover and explore your gifts. Experience them with your heart and soul. Feel the pleasure and wonder of their expression. Create your own moments, live with individuality, and be yourself.

Your gifts are yours. Own them and give them life, then share them with others. You may look to others for a better understanding of who you are, but do not emulate them for the sake of "fitting in." Justice would not be done if you were to live the life of another.

Your life is yours — an empty stage, a blank screen — with you as the artist. You are free to create what you want. Always remember the vast potential with which you have been blessed.

— Nancy Somers Dougherty

As Your Parent,
I Can't Promise You...

That things will always be rosy,
or that your skies will always be blue.
That there will be answers to all
    of your questions, or that your
    dreams will all come true.
That difficulties won't arise,
or that life will always be fair.
That your kindnesses will return to you,
or that your choices will always be clear.
That success in life will come easily,
or that happiness will stay by your side.
Or that everyone else will appreciate
    the special person you are inside.

But I Can Promise You...

That I'm very proud to be
  the parent of such a special person.
And — no matter what — I know you'll
  always make it through.

I'll always feel lucky to have
  you as a son.

And I'll always be here... loving you.

— Casey Whilson

When Problems Overwhelm You, Son, Here's a Little Poem for You to Remember...

Carry On

Carry on as I would, Son.
Lay your problems down to rest.
Put all bad times behind you
and strive to be your best.

Carry on with confidence;
your hands now hold the reins.
Don't think your talents won't compare,
for my blood runs through your veins.

Carry on with honesty;
you know what's right and fair.
Just call on me when problems strike;
you know that I'll be there.

Carry on the dream, my son.
Let your conscience be your guide.
Remember when you feel alone,
I'm standing by your side.

— Shelley McDaniel

My Son, Always Stay
the Unique Individual
That You Are

Men are told by society that
they must always be strong
They are told to block out
all sensitive, "unmanly" feelings
Men are told that
they must be leaders
they must achieve
they must succeed in a career
They are judged their whole lives
by the power they have
and how much money they earn

My son, I hope you will never
feel pressured by society
You should be free to think
and do whatever you want
and to act the way you feel at all times
You should cry when you want to
and laugh when you want to
You should just be
the outstanding person
that you are —
the person that I am so proud of
and whom I love always

— Susan Polis Schutz

"You Can Go as Far as Your Dreams Can Take You"

If you can reach out, you can hold on.
If you can imagine, you can achieve.
If you just begin, you can continue.
Search within, and you'll find a reason to believe.

If you can get involved, you can make it happen.
If you can give, you will be rewarded with the taking.
If you can climb, you can climb even higher.
Envision it; your success is in the making.

If you trust the winner within you, you will win.
If you can keep your courage, you will go so far.
If you follow your ambitions, your course will guide you
towards a ladder that you can climb to your stars.

If you don't put limits on yourself,
you can always keep striving.
You might amaze yourself with what
you discover you can do.
If you want to reach out for happiness,
don't ever forget these words:

You can go as far as your dreams can take you.

— Collin McCarty

In life, there will always be
   many paths to follow;
I hope you always choose
   the right one.

If you give
   a part of yourself to life,
the part you receive back
   will be so much greater.
Never regret the past,
   but learn by it.
Never lose sight of your dreams;
a person who can dream
   will always have hope.
Believe in yourself;
   if you do, everyone else will.
You have the ability
   to accomplish anything,
but never do it at
   someone else's expense.
If you can go through life
   loving others,
you will have achieved
the greatest success of all.

— Judy LeSage

I have loved
watching you go through life
as only a child can...
    laughing, crying,
    so sure of yourself,
and at the same time
    so often full of doubts.
My heart broke for you
    when life was unfair;
I would have shielded you
from pain and heartache
    if you had let me.

I wanted to protect you,
but you needed to grow
into your own person,
so I had to let go of you —
a little at a time.
That was one of the hardest
things I've ever had to do.

Your childhood is gone now,
    and I still miss those
        wonderful times,
but I am so proud of
the adult you have become.
I love you,
and whatever paths in life
you may choose to embrace,
    my love will be with you...
and I will cherish you always.

— Peggy Selig

Always Be True to Yourself, My Son, for There Is Greatness Within You

Throughout your life, I hope you will always
pursue sensitivity and kindness
    as your chosen way.
Your sense of humor is wonderful;
    hold on to it.
Being able to laugh at the world
    will see you through many hard times.
Guard against bitterness and sarcasm;
    they can destroy you.
Be yourself; the world will benefit
    from your talent and your humor.
Search for people who love and
    appreciate you for who you are
and who encourage you to improve.
Don't be satisfied with less
    than all you can be,
for you have greatness within you.

— Bill Cross

ACKNOWLEDGMENTS

The following is a partial list of authors whom the publisher especially wishes to thank for permission to reprint their works.

Katherine J. Romboldi for "I'll Always Care About Your Happiness." Copyright © 1994 by Katherine J. Romboldi. All rights reserved. Reprinted by permission.

M. Joye for "There was always something special...." Copyright © 1994 by M. Joye. All rights reserved. Reprinted by permission.

Nancye Sims for "Be Yourself!" Copyright © 1994 by Nancye Sims. All rights reserved. Reprinted by permission.

Lisa Hellermann for "Don't Ever Give Up on Your Dreams" by Vicki Silvers. Copyright © 1994 by Vicki Silvers. All rights reserved. Reprinted by permission.

Barbara J. Hall for "Work Hard, Son... but Have Fun, Too" and "Never Underestimate Your Abilities." Copyright © 1994 by Barbara J. Hall. All rights reserved. Reprinted by permission.

Tim Connor for "Make Every Day of Your Life an Adventure." Copyright © 1993 by Tim Connor. All rights reserved. Reprinted by permission.

Chris Marie Perrin for "As You Go Through Life, Son...." Copyright © 1994 by Chris Marie Perrin. All rights reserved. Reprinted by permission.

Jeffrey K. Lucas for "If Someone Asked Me to Define the Perfect Son, I Would Say...." Copyright © 1994 by Jeffrey K. Lucas. All rights reserved. Reprinted by permission.

Dena Dilaconi for "It's All Up to You, Son, to Make Your Dreams Come True." Copyright © 1994 by Dena Dilaconi. All rights reserved. Reprinted by permission.

Nancy Somers Dougherty for "Son, You Are the Artist of Your Life." Copyright © 1994 by Nancy Somers Dougherty. All rights reserved. Reprinted by permission.

A careful effort has been made to trace the ownership of poems used in this anthology in order to obtain permission to reprint copyrighted materials and give proper credit to the copyright owners. If any error or omission has occurred, it is completely inadvertent, and we would like to make corrections in future editions provided that written notification is made to the publisher:
    BLUE MOUNTAIN PRESS, INC., P.O. Box 4549, Boulder, Colorado 80306.

If you are interested in submitting your original poetry to Blue Mountain Press for possible inclusion in a future anthology, please write for guidelines or send your work with SASE to: BMA Editorial Department, P. O. Box 1007, Dept. BP, Boulder, Colorado 80306.